About the Author

Susie Meserve grew up outside of Boston and was educated at Tufts University and the University of Massachusetts at Amherst. Her poems have appeared in *Indiana Review, Cimarron Review, Bateau, Gulf Coast*, and others. She is also the author of the chapbook *Faith* (Finishing Line Press). She lives in Berkeley, California, with her husband and two young sons.

Little Prayers

Poems

by

Susie Meserve

BLUE LIGHT PRESS ◆ 1ST WORLD PUBLISHING

SAN FRANCISCO ◆ FAIRFIELD ◆ DELHI

Winner of the 2018 Blue Light Book Award

Little Prayers

Copyright ©2018 by Susie Meserve

All rights reserved. Printed in the United States of America. No part of this book may be used or reproduced in any manner whatsoever without written permission except in the case of brief quotations embodied in critical articles and reviews. For information contact:

1st World Library
PO Box 2211
Fairfield, IA 52556
www.1stworldpublishing.com

Blue Light Press
www.bluelightpress.com
bluelightpress@aol.com

Book & Cover Design
Melanie Gendron
melaniegendron999@gmail.com

Cover Art
Melanie Gendron

Author Photo
Kelly Lynn James

First Edition

Library of Congress Control Number: 2018931571

ISBN 9781421838021

For Ben
for Leo
for Sam

CONTENTS

Against Prophecy 11

PART ONE: FLYING DREAMS

A Bird, A God 17
Mysterious Building 18
October 20
Bus Driver 21
Crop 23
Barn 24
Boundary Music 25
The First Hour 26
Time Difference 27
Steps To Get Over 28
Field Study 29
Losing Paradise 30
The Trouble with Foreign Languages 31
Powder 32
Rêve 33
Expecting Airplanes 34
Science 35
Flying Dream 36
Still Life 37
Song 38
Is It Like This for You? 39
Night 40

PART TWO: AGAINST PROPHECY

On Living 43
Diary 44
Summertime 45
San Francisco 46
Fog 47
Little Elegy 50
Tell Me Everything 51
First God Made 52
Overlook 53
Soon, Then 54
Love Poem 55
Return to California 56
True Story 57
The Stars & The Planets 58
Statement of Plans 59
The Village Elder 60
Blooming 61
Mistaken Identity 62
For My Unborn Niece 63
Doing Dishes 64
Little Prayer 65
Belation 66
On the Last Day 67
The Oracle 68

Acknowledgments 71

I put this book here for you, who once lived
So that you should visit us no more.

—Czeslaw Milosz, from "Dedication"

AGAINST PROPHECY

Don't tell me
Nostradamus saw it coming,
that a goateed stranger

with the wherewithal to change a tire in hailstones
might knock at my apartment
in the next ten days. Don't foresee for me, please,

the Lithium bottle carefully shortening
night table's distance to bedside,
the mother taking shape in the vinegar bottle,

the last grievous letter from California.
Give me the log in the forest, that, lifted,
reveals a nest of snakes,

their heads shying from the light,
vertebrae called sluggishly
to attention.

LITTLE PRAYERS

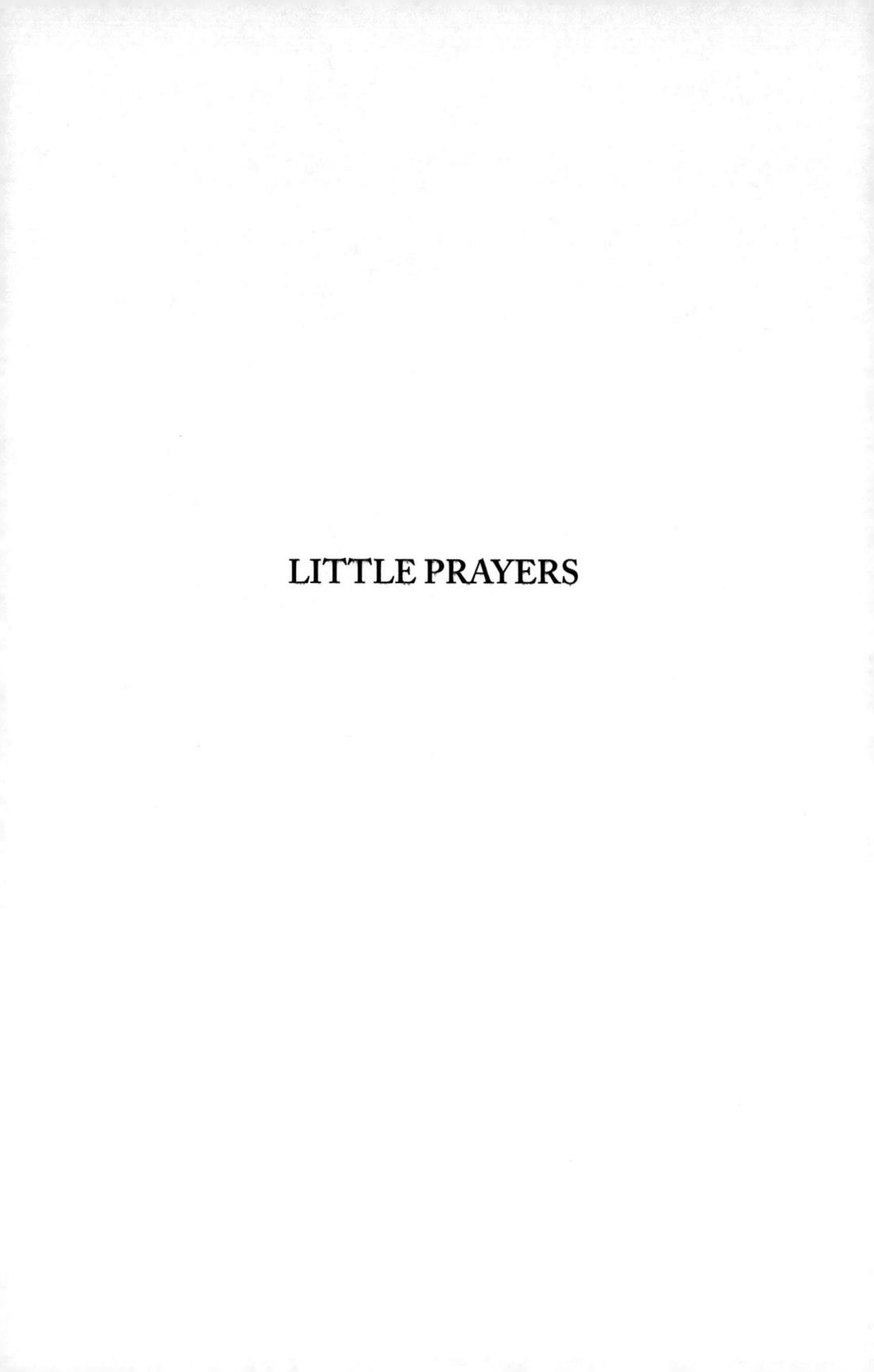

Part One: Flying Dreams

A BIRD, A GOD

I've been holding something
in my hard fat belly for days
and in the night I wake from dark dreams.
But no one, nothing, is there.
A bird, a God, what was it you saw last?
Was it this?
I've forgotten how to read, what language
to pluck from the ears of strangers.
I salute the sun facing a dead blue wall.
I look into the earth.
Were you a tree cutter? Is that how you knew,
by looking into the mouths of trees?

MYSTERIOUS BUILDING

There it is, the blood
of the hummingbird who, mistaking sky,
flew into the living room
and fluttered there like a fish
out of water — stupid thing —
no sense to stop batting out its life
against my window.
This was my gift: the hummingbird's beak,
scissored and wordlessly shouting.
I had never seen one so close or so slow,
not needle-dipping into a fuchsia
faster than my eye could follow.
And this was my burden: to stop
its death. Later, a friend
said *what a good omen*, a bird
(especially hummer, colibri, oiseau-mouche)
to fly into my living room.
What grace. And all those bones,
10,000 bones to try
not to break. I could not take myself
so seriously, terrified as it,
hands like crushing clumsy paws
but I held it held it held it *held it!* —
and brought it to the gap
where sun streamed in,
Friday afternoon, the fog not yet rolled up
in great billows from the ocean.

And let it go.
I failed; it batted some more,
hit the window again, chewing air.
No sound; it never made any sound.
Finally, it found the space
and swam off. Three spots
on the napkin. Red, like mine.

OCTOBER

It's raining colored paper.
No, birds — cardinals, orioles, and canaries,
swooping, dipping toward the hard surface
of the road, then gone. It's the cornfields

have turned to paper, and a pumpkin's
split its head on a front stoop.
A boy discovers it and starts to cry.
Who would *do* such a thing,

bring down the jagged grin, hard, on the steps?
Something in him falters.
He imagines his house on fire: water boiling
in the goldfish bowl, his floating, weightless fish.

He thinks of God and Judas
and seventeen-year locusts, how they ruin things,
wringing his hands, his fingernails
in splinters. He stares at the fields,

counts minutes till schooltime, his breath
a neat circle on the window,
because it's cold this October, already —
and there in the road is the flock of leaves,

swooping, dipping into the hard surface,
then gone. They touch down, and then they're gone.
The cornfields have turned to paper.
Behind them, the sky.

BUS DRIVER

He did an unexpected thing,
turned off Route 9 onto a side street,
and tooled us around a corner
where we took flight, the bus sprouting

great wings, houses like push pins
on a map, all the places we could go.
And the light — O September!
Like honey, like marble, like amber, champagne,

rolling down the sides of the bus —
will it ever stop making me want to die?
New England houses in shades of drab,
their white trim, their ghosts, a crocus bed,

and then, in a backyard, a roof-mounted
Jovian moon. *Surprise.*
(Somehow like peeking in
on a sleeping child

when you'd forgotten he existed,
alive, his breathing reckless,
his knees akimbo,
wallpaper sailboats bobbing peacefully

in the night.) But the detour —
it didn't help. Still on the side road
the cars stacked up like cakes
and the light began to fail, crepuscular cicadas

never bothering to sing.
When we flew past the Ristorante Aqua Vitae
the head waiter thrust his head out the window,
looking to the sky as though waiting

on Pompeii's ashes or a dish of pasta
gone missing from the kitchen,
waiting for linguine to lift off the plate
like hair stands up on a jumping body.

There is so much living left to do, damn it,
we never get off easy,
so when I see this waiter lean
out the window — when I see linguine

flop back down on the plate —
I want, too, to see Pompeii's ashes
swirling down, baptism
on the satellite dish,

so inside the house
the television sparks out,
and our bus slowly becomes covered,
too early for snow, we'll all think,

but it's so gorgeous, the way the sky
clouds over: snow on the peony heads, snow
on the corn fields, and close to the end, snow
on the slice of moon reflecting dead water.

CROP

Burning brush off Route 116,
farmers stand around in overalls,
keeping things under control. God was there,
too. All day, God — in the market
as I place apples in a brown bag,
as I thank the wind for being low.
Last night I saw God too, I suppose,
but who can tell? I hate the waiting.
The farmers have been waiting all day.
This is conjecture; I've long since driven past.
I'm on my way home to make a list:
1) Put away apples;
2) Get over sexual hang-ups;
3) Walk dog —
But all day I've been smelling smoke.
Now I'm imagining a wagonload of books,
eating an apple and noticing that perfect contrast
of fibrous red skin and fleshy white insides,
the taste like a fusillade, *bang*.
I pull brown pits
from the core, think of planting a tree…
if I choke down some soil,
will an apple tree grow in me?
I'd love those Cox's Orange Pippins!
Or perhaps I'd grow tired
of the trunk in my esophagus,
the leaves ticklish and scratchy,
the fruit of dubious quality.

BARN

Two skies: one backlit, blue.
The dark one contains the moon.

Moon! Moon! Moon! Moon! Moon!

It's night, of course.
Summer feels arbitrary, but not impossible:
the red barn five miles north might be
in Tennessee, or not a barn at all. But I like it

in a way I can't know, driving past, where
there's a harness, a horse, or even an inside.

BOUNDARY MUSIC

No moon to speak of. I've come

to love the leaves when they crumble this way,

coffee grounds on the running path

and all the apples ready for next season.

Radioactive pumpkins in a paper field.

Why does this landscape make me

put my palm over one eye

and pray to disappear?

I'll be caught between seasons.

I'll refuse to say goodbye.

Like these squashes here:

intact until you flip them broadside

to reveal a nest of maggots

trying to devour

a washboard of seeds.

THE FIRST HOUR

When I'm still, the light
glows like egg yolk flown in
from another state.
The mind reaches to imagine
Minnesota, Wisconsin, The Dakotas,
where a woman pulls on her snow pants
to fetch the paper down the road.
Whereas it's dry here, and unseasonably warm.

But let me die in springtime
clutching a fistful of helium balloons,
the life of the maple groaning
in its buds, and I will not long
for somewhere else. No,
I will not long at all.

Today, a subterranean spiraling
and up come crocus,
as the cars park and repark
and we trundle on in the unfailing sun.

God help us, it's February.
Appearing, now: birds.

TIME DIFFERENCE

It's snowing but not accumulating
And everyone leaves the laundromat
With more than they brought.
Daylight savings has screwed things up:
Coffee shops open late, bread refuses to rise,
Alarm clocks around town play
"If I Were a Bell" in unison,
Then in a round, now a slow fugue, then a fade to silence
While the snow comes down.
We hear of a plane crash in Taipei
The morning before it's happened, and how tragic:
Dead on a Wednesday when it's not yet Wednesday.
And where do those bodies go?
There must be no seasons there: sometimes cold,
Mostly mild, usually dry, sometimes a hint of rain.
Nights are cloudless, starless, moonless,
At dawn a violet light. A tiny hiccup
On Solstice. Bicycles are winged
And if you're lucky
You can cross the dateline in a day.
The international agreement is called off.
You learn to obey streetlights, caffeinate to keep up —
But few make it, and fewer make it back,
They climb too close to the sun,
They fall to the sharks and the Kraken.
When you wash ashore, your unisuit is slit
From crotch to neck, both halves burned.
Then they untangle the sand
From your hair, peer beneath your fingernails,
Roll back the eyes in your head, and you wait.

STEPS TO GET OVER

Again the wind rose & shook the leaves off
The trees throw shadows on the sidewalk
We trudge along avoiding each other
Because sometimes everyone is the enemy even
The guy in the trench coat & black hat lingers over the box
Where they keep the free newspapers taking one out
At the ballpark a baseball took off through
The stratosphere was pierced by a comet with rough edges
And a whole series of constellations you didn't know
How sharp I was I just got your letter & photograph
Thank you I treasure it as an artifact of the love that never
Was I too effusive or too
Odd how the baseball takes its arc from the moon
If the moon were a motion it would be whoosh
Go the leaves on the sidewalk in a sudden gust
That leaves us all
Breathless is how I felt when I got your letter
And tucked it into the drawer alongside other things
Aren't so good here since you last
Rote memory is a funny thing because it makes us
Crazies in the crosswalk & a marching band on the town hall
Steps to get over you are too numerous to mention here
Come the cheerleaders who arrived with the marching
Band & will leave on the shoulders of a hundred football players
Are birds of paradise whispering *play*
Secrets are not fun for the person who doesn't notice
The sidewalk dappled with leaf-shaped light
A cigarette in winter & it's a tiny planet in your fingers

FIELD STUDY

After a snow, blind fingers clutch
another universe. This one: drifts

on a rooftop, dusted awning across the street,
powder throat-high in the gooseneck of a streetlamp.

Write me — tell me your latitude and longitude,
how it looks there, the traffic patterns

and the flight delays. And have the rains
started, have they stopped? It's snowed here —

I mentioned that — and I pore over field notes,
two absent-minded spoons in the coffee.

Temperature. Noiselessness. Quality of Clumping.
Depth and Precision of Snow-angel.

Hundreds of them lay down in the field last night,
arced their wings overhead, and took off.

LOSING PARADISE

And then it was Christmas,
and what had we done all year?

There was loss — there is always
loss — and there will be other losses —

Sometimes we got drunk alone.
It felt so true, like walking away

with someone else's hand.
And sometimes we knew to kill

what needed killing, folding the wings
against the heat of the still body,

over the dark heart.
Sometimes we put things in a paper bag

and shook and shook them up:
an alligator, a moon, the femoral curve of a leg.

Intractable, our sadness, heroic, our defeat,
we forgave ourselves our trespasses,

vowed to start again. A tree went up in the parlor,
an angel alight on the crest.

THE TROUBLE WITH FOREIGN LANGUAGES

Too bad the day's so gray
or we'd put a quarter in the viewfinder
and look for Mars, gray planet.
Martian towers aren't as fine as this, wrought iron
and steel and pressure-treated four-by-eights

now gilded with pixilated crystals of ice,
the kind you long to touch your tongue to
spasmodically, illogically, as one rears
toward the head of Medusa and ends up
similarly fucked. If the sky were Chinese

characters it would say something unintelligible
but in English it's strato-nimbus-cumulus-cirrus,
in German *reinkalttrübunbekannt*,
pure cold cloudy unknown.
And in Russian, my Love — O my love, my love.

POWDER

In Egypt the pharaohs found it snowing
and decried every pictograph declaring sun.
They threw their support to the cumulus Gods
and their decades of bluster, of hardworn storefronts,
tattered awnings, long dark mornings, and unseasonable
cold. They portended spring. They portended
the snow angels. And the wind, rattling the sideboard.

In the end they found a footpath, littered
with broken gauze and secrets.
It led to the conservatory, where above
the crowned succulents, between the ceiling-high
palms, around the ladder they drove through the roof
in despair of something more botanical breaking

through, the pharaohs chose vertigo,
and dizzying heights, and the way
when the snow swirled it assumed
a shape like a pyramid, each flake a block,
and each block a star, each star a three-foot drift,
the footpath whited out, powder up to the crook,
and it could not follow and would not stop.

RÊVE

Long after you dreamed the leaves fell
in the living room and a pharaoh arrived
to rake them up, you woke to a phosphorescent glow
like the low city lights from far out in the ocean,
or like shining a flashlight in through your mouth
to light a cavern in the fat of your cheeks. Your friends
loved how you rolled your eyes back, waving
around with the one free arm, then Jasper put the light
under his sweatshirt and said *E.T. phone home.*
It was your birthday party. You wanted the pirate ship
and a Hoodsie cup, the radiator clanged,
and someone handed you a cupcake —

Later, years later

when the leaves were falling and the city
turned to streetlights you felt like a canoe
passing silently into fog on a still lake.
The hills peeked out orange and red and yellow,
this was your home, you knew precisely the color
the leaves would turn before they dropped,
and the trees reached their bare fingers into the dying sky.

EXPECTING AIRPLANES

Sweet Kate, you've just been born,
and the clouds write your name above the garden.
I look up hearing airplanes but it's just the traffic
and the lilies, the pinkest of Chinese maples.

The pink is going away.

I've grown anxious
the stars too might burn out,
topple over and off into the sea,
tossing the ocean in great sheets.

I feel sad about this.

But give me the moment the Pacific starts to churn!
Let me look down from a Chinese kite,
my tail a thousand silver fish. Fish in the sky,
fish in the sea, and all the rugosas exiled.

SCIENCE

I was scared to expose the underside of a leaf
and let a child run over it with skinny fingers
knowing he might fall in love or he might shred the leaf
into triangles and scatter them like seed.

Every time I open my mouth, something hops in.

The child was at my party.
We stood blithe amid confetti and streamers,
ice cubes and cheese straws. We twirled our drink stirrers
around our tongues, wrapped them in awkward bows.
A bath overflowed down the stairs
and out the front door, crossed the fields,
joined with the sea, and swept out.

Loops of suds gathered in the stair beds. We couldn't go down or up.

One day I'm a straight line. The next, a star.
The next, I'm the broken glass that cuts a cylinder
from another woman's face and puts it on,
praying for the graft to take.

FLYING DREAM

Sailing low,
weightless, quiet, the hood
of my sweatshirt lifting
about my ears like a halo, I knew
to flex my right arm ceilingward
and cry out when I approached the staircase,
spiraled and dark —

    I am no angel,
my heart thumped in its lonely hollow,
soaring above the piano and its pink vase
of tulips

Approaching the cupola, I floated
in tepid air, swimming at the knees
and hips

Oh koi in the pond outside,
blink at me through the picture window

STILL LIFE

A sparrow landed in the space
between storm and outer pane,
fluttered there spastic,
tiring itself out while I considered
what to do. I readied a hand towel.
I imagined holding back the wings,
warm shape firm as a grapefruit,
a sense I'd done this in a past life,
muscle memory vivid as the bird itself,
its terrible beak, its terrible eyes
trained on everything but me —
then knowing I'd not held
a wild animal before,
that it wouldn't feel
like I wanted it to.

She broke out.
Confused where to find the sky,
she landed on the lampshade.
Almost camouflaged, still life
of dresser and sparrow.
When I approached
with the towel she vaulted
for the now-open window.
How transparent my relief
when she'd gone. I could still feel
her release from my hands.

SONG

Late light brings the trees so close
they almost silence
the album you recommended,
your way to believe I hear what you hear.

I've been dancing and swinging
my pretend red hair while quietly, quietly,
night has lifted up the sky.
What does the light do in California,

as you ash your smoke on the porch?
I've consulted the love songs of the ages.
None can explain why I want to be
your cigarette on its return trip

from your mouth.
The day's gone by.
A pink and violet fire
kisses the mountain.

I miss you backwards.
Your name sings to me:
la la la la la.

IS IT LIKE THIS FOR YOU?

Daytime in the city I'm invisible
but the sky's still blue. More than that —
the clouds drift like letters from an old friend
once loved: magical, a little unsettling,
forgotten in the shoebox, mostly white.

Bedtime I discovered one such letter
and dreamed of the friend in her kitchen.
She made toast and wrote a note — *deceased,
no forwarding address* — on a slip of paper
I lost in a snow bank when I shut the door.

But how was it before? Did we idle
at stoplights chewing our fingernails, pondering
buoyancy, unaware that planes could drop like acorns?
Fall is still my favorite season. Unconscionable
how lovely, and not just the sky.

When I die tomorrow I will not have uttered
my last words. I will call to say
I love you, but you don't write or
I still concede you were wrong or
My greatest mistake was failing to shout your name.

NIGHT

Strange rumbling, an ache
where once there were
no aches. Insatiable thirst,
the taste of jonquils on my tongue.
Small fire in my bones. It lights
my way down the hall, burns out.

Someday soon
I will swathe myself in scarves,
in gloves and hats and quilts and coats
then lie down to roast
like a succulent, tremulous bird.

Part Two: Against Prophecy

ON LIVING

Some mornings you look forward
To the toothbrush. Others you grumble,
Grinding the familiar old beans
That save you from indolence,
The way a cold beer, multiplied, saves you
From making good decisions,
And a spliff, smoked in the back seat
Of the car, saves you
From *really addressing your anger.*
So the circus goes:
Sunday midnight the band next door
Holds practice, their drums beginning
As raindrops, ending as typhoon,
Eclipsing all thought but what to do
About the fruitflies? They've taken over
The fruit bowl, now the fridge, appearing
Yesterday as dark floating lint in the closet,
Underwear drawer, flying out of the shower
When you turned it on. And how many times
Did you stub your toe on the *Book of Ruth*
Before you learned to pick it up? Lying there
Pondering The Fruitfly Conundrum, you imagine
Strep throat coming unannounced; love, maybe.
Maxims float in, song lyrics attach,
Next thing you know you're humming "Crazy"
Under the covers at three in the afternoon,
A pipe that hasn't clanged in forty years
Commences to clanging, you have a sudden craving
For grits, and gunshots shatter the road.

DIARY

Today on the streetcar I felt not as buoyant
as I once was. Like a woman wearing a wig.
No; like a woman *looking into* wearing a wig,
not sure whether to go platinum or atomic.

•

I like new things. But anchovies
cannot replace milk. Fountain pens adorned with gold
should not substitute for pencils. Lead comforts. Lead
reminds us of our school days. Pink erasers? Even better.

•

It's been ages since I made a list.

It would go sea urchin, hummock, cast iron skillet with handle.

You see? Once it was *balloons, balloons, balloons.*

SUMMERTIME

I would stomp porcelain teacups,
sprinkle them with powdered wasabi, crying
Japanese for horseradish, Japanese for horseradish —
This isn't, strictly speaking, accurate, but how
lovely the celadon, like quails' eggs, ground.

And what did nakedness ever get us but fear
the window shade wasn't drawn all the way?
We wear earrings to hearken back.
When we floss, spaces that were filled
become unfilled. Unfilled is beautiful.

Teeth are like corn cobs, only harder.
Petrified cobs, then. The field is filled with them,
and with early bees — stars — luminaria —
In my kingdom there will be bees.
We'll mold rings out of honey

and though sightless they will clatter
into the dish above the sink as hands
start warming and wetting plates,
rinsing plates, stacking plates in upright rows,
putting away plates in cupboards.

A slow filling, like an unfilling, is beautiful.
And cicadas, forsythia, the lilac.

SAN FRANCISCO

This city is like a cache for thieves. And with the traffic stopped, as skeletal. I find it best in this light, its rafters strung with early magnolia. Weeks later, the tatters lie in fragrant shreds. They turn brown and clog the sidewalks. Who will sweep them up?

This city ended once. In summer, the light's gray and the tree filaments tangle in high winds. The sun is a fickle visitor. The park fills with all sorts: they read books, they comfort children, they wrestle dogs.

I asked for faith in this city. It had rained again, and the sky seeped water like a wound. Faith didn't come. I found myself pacing, thinking I had a picture somewhere, that a stranger would make it materialize. He smiled, he pointed to churches, but he didn't know faith.

My lover and I knew cities: we slept in parks on warm afternoons, waiting for trains and no place to screw. We walked through palaces, pictured ourselves king. Once we stole across a fence.
In a high garden, the city bubbled like a fountain below us.

Today I took a jog in the park. The sky was suspended by strings.

FOG

[Morning]

The raven-haired beauty with apricot hips
sits with her coffee, reads.
It's a false cool day.
A fog is coming in.
In the café the cook fries bacon,
roasts beans, builds heat —
and Ravenhair gets up to go.
I wish she would not. I like her curls.
But she flies away,
down Geary Boulevard,
against the thickening sky.

[Fog]

I would like to view it under a microscope,
smoosh the sputtering droplets
between glass.
Fog is only different from mist,
reads the encyclopedia,
for its density. Thick sheets close off
Marin, hide the East Bay,
obscure the Presidio.
Above which:
a bushy canopy of green,
somewhere a road,
and a gray grove of eucalyptus.

[Noon]

Horn moans low over stones and sea.
I wonder where it lives?
Oh and listen, there are two —
one resplendent,
one faint,
like port and starboard
or a near-and-far galaxy.
I want the distant one
to wrap its long voice across the waves,
cross this ocean,
and sing me to sleep.

[Lust]

The man in the coffee shop, newly awake:
*I wonder what it would be like to live
above something.* The law, I think,
or dew point. But he means a store or a deli.
I think sea level and the 39th parallel,
Hades, or the pinnacle
where lightning begins to crack.
Perhaps he means Ravenhair,
hips anchored beneath him,
a thousand Corvus coraces
winging across his pillow.

[Dusk]

Waves collide. The lighthouse is shrouded. The man there flinches from ships. Even the gulls have stopped wheeling; the seas are too high. Night, night, oh morning.

[Fog]

I want to have a good day,
thought Ravenhair, disappearing
into the curtain on Clement Street.

I want to have a good day,
thought the man, wondering
how she would look in his bed.

I want to have a good day,
prayed the lighthouse attendant
as night became morning

and through a break in the curtain
he saw land,
sea,

and a ship passing through.
I have a voice after all.
I will sing to you from my tower.

LITTLE ELEGY
for Shahid

I think of you like ball-peen hammers,

tinkling in a hall of mirrors.

Like the fog horn on a clear day.

•

In that box — so close I thought to leap up in my skirt and hat

and wrench off the lid — I wondered if death was abrupt.

Like wind, seizing a house.

But you, poet, rolled off without a hitch.

•

I have murdered you, friend.

In spring I'll shake snow off the bulbs,

say prayers for your cashmere, your postcards,

your flutes. For oboes and jazz trombones.

Your ghosts flit about the house.

Only you, darling, would have more than one.

TELL ME EVERYTHING

I would grasp your shoulders like a yoke
and ride you into the start of something.

How would it be to feel so useful?

And write a short book about the time you broke
your collarbone in three places,

your eyes on morphine green, unafraid, almost unseeing.
I think I'll make up some words today, one to describe

yellow and orange and red trees in fog from the bus window,
one to replace *lonesome*,

one for mornings I hate to get up but do so knowing
it's what humans do when the world's a-light,

and love's a thousand miles in the wrong direction.

FIRST GOD MADE

Wind or something else
that enters quietly, breathing.

Funny to see this city dusted in snow,
sanguine, contiguous. I miss

when skies are gray and you come knocking in,
your limbs like streetlamps.

How is my heart when you put it down
like a box of lightbulbs?

I think of the girl who caught a cold
through the phone. She believed

microbes could swim in air two cities
apart. If love could swim

a thousand cities apart, like lights
slowly catching on a cord —

both parties would wind up raspy,
holding a tin can with a string.

OVERLOOK

The terrain staggers me: scapula,
skull, the place his heart
does its thing. Is there God at 42,000 feet?
I smile at the child who kicks
my chair. His mother thanks me
for my patience. If I pray,
it's to return. Overlook of houses —
where is he now, what shadow
have I left in his bed? Is it like the shadow
an airplane casts taking me away,
the one made by an ascending plane?
I am not patient.
I like miracles: flowers stand up,
flowers fall down.

SOON, THEN

But miracles are for other people.
Here it grows humid

and we stop watering the garden.
Earth crumbles at the base of an eggplant.

Because who declared a weed a weed? And what if God
is a criminal? If God made hands, God made ghosts.

Hands would run right through ghosts.
Ghost speared by hand, hand surrounded by ghost,

both feeling just a slight warmth, a gentle rocking.
Like a love poem, perhaps, or ending a letter with soon, then.

LOVE POEM

The running path in the woods
near the college, and a man
asking me not to slap at mosquitoes
because they're just mothers

feeding their young. Until then,
there existed no parallel between my life
and the man's. I slap them, now, I kill them
on summer days. We are not lovers.

It never even started; I have married someone else.
But I still have a book,
Dickinson's letters,
a green paperback I am guilty of keeping,

inadvertently
or not. I could not live with him.
It was summer. Every other weekend
I drove to Maine to see my family.

He didn't believe in cars, or family.
His thoughts struck me as skittish.
I didn't know to understate how he made
me feel. I believe I never made it beyond

his saying *being in love hurts as much
as falling out of love*. Even though he'd quit,
he enjoyed a cigarette on his balcony sometimes.
I ached when it left his mouth.

RETURN TO CALIFORNIA

They have violins there
and the sky can be shattered with a small pick.
There is faith, there is faith, there is faith.

The canopies of trees sprout other trees.
It's like climbing a circus tent
to find the Serengeti, and none of the lions

know about the ringmaster or the cotton candy.
Sometimes in California we chat by telephone
while waving across the room at each other, that old joke.

We speak sign language under water. The words
seem blurry. In California the plan has flown
out the window. The window is a sheet of glass.

It's hard to imagine a world without fog.

TRUE STORY

We took the glass elevator to the sun —
there is, as you've imagined,

a lizard there, barely pulsing,
tongue engaged, tail poised to snap

and bleed. This would explain
the light today,

lizard-shaped and chasing itself
in great comical circles

around the living room. And the signals
interfering with the radio,

a crackling like grackles in the winesap,
like squirrels dropping their teacups

on an old tin roof.
The furniture has stood up on its own

two legs and demanded audience.
Let's listen.

THE STARS & THE PLANETS

I felt surprised to learn you too
stood beneath a grape arbor and the sky
was about to lift up its lid and shoot off,
leaving us in blackness.
Sometimes my dreams are for shit, but I love you.
All night, the grape leaves shuffling
in the wind, three a.m., four,
on into the morning — *did I wake you?* No —
Did you dream about wine? *Me too* —

Always your voice, the finest of trellises,
the raspberries have gone by,
you say, *don't forget your ticket*, you say,
I'll drive you home.
And the next night, and the next,
and the night after that,
the stars up there, sure, being watched.

STATEMENT OF PLANS

I know you cannot know
how to bind with such fine string.
It is breaking. Outside, the fall maples
in their yellow leaves, a bright truck,
a nascent film crew taking shots
in the garden of roses.
I have walked in circles not round enough.
I have always considered the pale heart.
But some things,
like love, subsume others. You look
away, you take a letter from a friend
and let it drop. Each time I get it wrong.

Oh to be so steadfast, drawing up these plans.

THE VILLAGE ELDER

He woke to a thousand gravestones,
windows opening one after another
like a moth batting out its life on a lit bulb.
He rose in silence,
cemetery receding as in a noir film,
but what is the point of an old movie in new times?

He didn't tell me

how the window caught light:
headstone, epigraph, vase
of paper roses, moss. I'd lost
the little slips of paper, misplaced
the stones to my heart.
I wanted to lean against the cloth of his beard
and with my fingers, find his mouth.

BLOOMING

I've moved the jasmine to the bedroom.

Waking, baroque blossoms — too petite for such scent — yellow
leaves, and webworm binding its stems. I bring my fingers

to the cloud. Such nothingness. Like blood,
or the truck that stops in the night, waits in the shadow

of a gas pump, cargo untouched. But like blood,
when it arrives: brown washboard in the sheets, quick spill

from the hand taking down the broken window.

MISTAKEN IDENTITY

The leaves quake in their sockets.
It's been raining all night,

and a platoon of mosquitoes has pitched
from gossamer bubbles, afterbirths floating,

too tiny for the eye, in the puddle
collecting on the deck. I would swim that puddle.

Shadow-shaped shadows on the lawn,
boulders slick with rain,

this long night becoming morning.
Someone has made off with the bird feeder.

FOR MY UNBORN NIECE

Sometimes I hear your voice
like a wind chime on a distant porch,
see your face as the sun, risen
but not yet moved to where I, turning
in sleep, will be awoken.

You come in pieces: skirt, hair, embryo, fire.
Once a man walked into the wood, came across
a child in a basket, picked it up and took it home.
I have been meaning to ask what happened
to that child, whether it outgrew the length

of its container. But we are what we are, sweet
nothing. We outgrow everything, even tears.
Soon you will be out of practice in being born.
You will walk down a street at night.
You will look up at the moon. *My children,*

you will think. *I have outgrown my children.*

DOING DISHES

I whir the Cuisinart blade like a propeller.
Happily, no one's around for my *vroom vroom*.
I think of other pointy objects: cacti & sea urchins,
not strictly objects because they live & breathe.
The plant is debatable but not that it lives
& that a gnome's hat is pointy, also not debatable.
I'll send you a list of pointy things,
pens & needles & witches & thistles.
The thistles by the Nile
are the earth from 10,000 miles.

LITTLE PRAYER

God grant me the serenity to work
things hard, and carefully.

I lie fallow between mountains.
I accept the things I cannot change.

God grant me the hamster wheel, fly wheel, nautilus.
Copper pipe with brass fittings.

God grant me the Mill River, all in a sheet
over the dam. Grant me the wide Connecticut

and everything that falls beneath it,
because it is fast, and silent,

and sometimes I feel breathless.

BELATION

Never is worse
than late,
so we hold on
to late.
We pay bills
past due,
mail gifts
after Christmas.
Easter Bunny
comes in July.
The crocuses bloom
in a hundred Octobers
and this we know
from our ghosts.

When I come back
I want to be the strings
binding your birthday,
the cross
and the loops,
unwound
with precision,
and lovingly
pulled through.

ON THE LAST DAY

I saw my grandmother wearing tulle
and a swarm of wasps
in sunshower over the catalpa —
all that gold made me hazy
and dry, a little giddy, so that asleep
seemed a wiser choice than awake.
Cardoso, plantain, meshugenah,
words like papillons rode by in slo-mo,
then fast-mo, as though getting it right
for what comes after:
the sweet feel of lips
against my neck, then my eyelids,
then my four limbs, imagined or real.

THE ORACLE

I was in Produce —
before I'd left the house — when I predicted
the toppling of Stonehenge and paid a phone bill
for 2021. I came to my senses in Frozen Foods,
before my senses had come to themselves.
Afternoon was worse; Doric grew Ionic,
hypothetical-cum-probable, ants traversed the shards
of sidewalk and carried off crumb after crumb.
Tonight through the yammering jackhammer
the disasters took ominous shape: an infidelity,
a wedding, an argument over zinnias
for the head table.

I didn't want to see these things.

I had a taste for an ancient recipe,
copied in meticulous hand into a small green book
with a thousand other details I meant to tell you:
the inscription on my grave, the location of the key,
the blueprints for the pantry and greenhouse.
They were all there.
But when I lifted the book the words fell
like petals from the pages,
and glowed for a minute at my feet.

ACKNOWLEDGMENTS

I am grateful to the editors of the following magazines, in which some of these poems have appeared, sometimes in subtle disguise:

The Café Review: Little Elegy
Cimarron Review: Steps to Get Over
Indiana Review: Time Difference; October
Redactions: Field Study; Overlook
Red Rock Review: Losing Paradise
Terminus: For My Unborn Niece
West-Northwest Journal of Environmental Law: Field Study
Willamette Week: Diary

The poem "Steps to Get Over" is after Matthea Harvey.

The last line of "Is It Like This for You?" owes a debt to Charles Simic's poem *"errata."*

The last line in the poem "The Stars & The Planets" is inspired by the Modest Mouse song "3rd Planet."

Thank you Samar Abulhassan, Michelle Bonczek Evory, Mike Dockins, Ben Eichenberg, Diane Frank, Melanie Gendron, Dawn Lundy Martin, and Dara Wier. In memory of Agha Shahid Ali, who reminded us that the world is full of paper. I wish I could still write to him.

CPSIA information can be obtained
at www.ICGtesting.com
Printed in the USA
LVOW12s1645140218
566599LV00001B/263/P